praisecharts

PLAYBACK+
Speed • Pitch • Balance • Loop

Contemporary Worship Classics

T0070483

CONTENTS

To access audio visit:
www.halleonard.com/mylibrary
Enter Code
2436-0832-7201-6359

ISBN 978-1-4950-3467-1

HAL•LEONARD®
CORPORATION
7777 W. BLUEMOUND RD. P.O. BOX 13819 MILWAUKEE, WI 53213

Visit Hal Leonard Online at
www.halleonard.com

www.praisecharts.com

Amazing Grace
(My Chains Are Gone)

B♭ Instruments

Words by John Newton
Traditional American Melody
Additional Words and Music by
Chris Tomlin and Louie Giglio
Arranged by Dan Galbraith

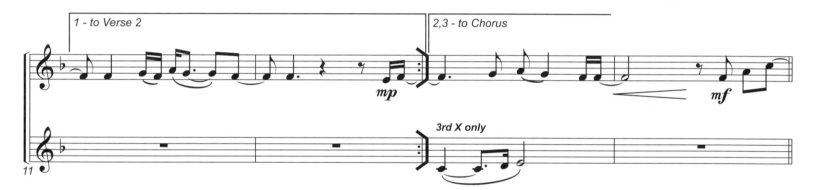

Forever

Bb Instruments

Words and Music by Chris Tomlin
Arranged by Dan Galbraith

3 Pre-Chorus *"Sing praise..."*

4 Chorus *"Forever God is..."*

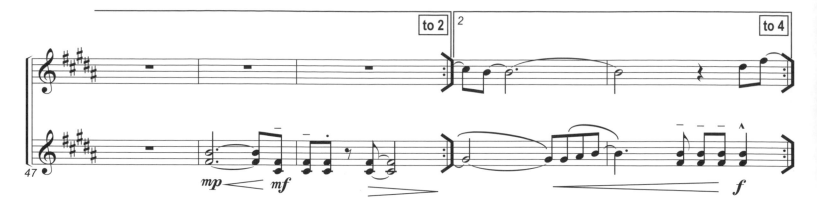

5 Bridge

"Give thanks to the Lord..."

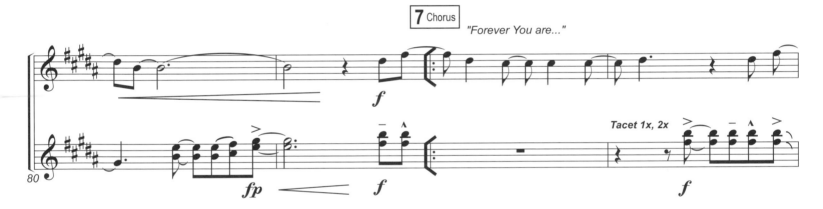

God of Wonders

Bb Instruments

Words and Music by Marc Byrd
and Steve Hindalong
Arranged by Dan Galbraith and Dave Iula

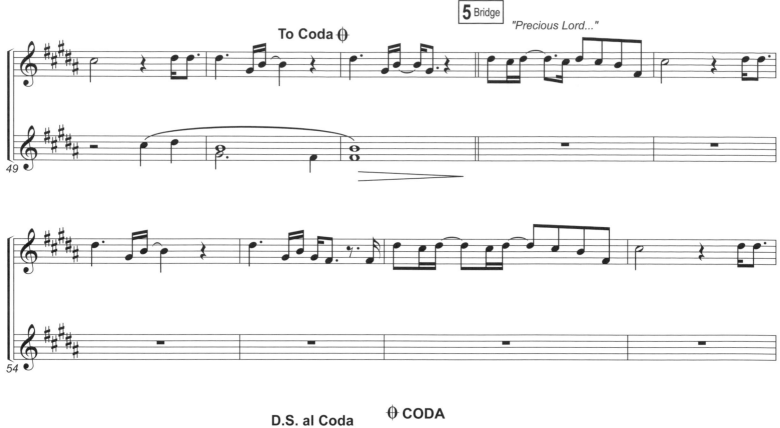

Blessed Be Your Name

Bb Instruments

Words and Music by Matt Redman
and Beth Redman
Arranged by Dan Galbraith and Shane Ohlson

Straight-ahead rock ♩ = 123

1 Verse
1. "Blessed....in the land..."
2. "Blessed...when the sun's..."

12

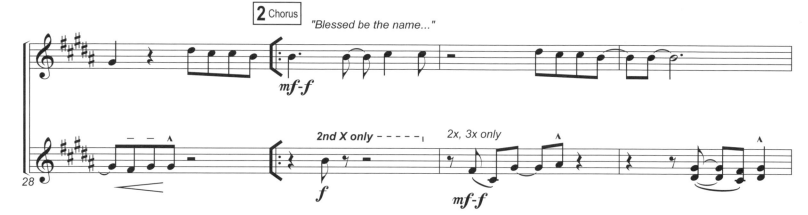

2 Chorus *"Blessed be the name..."*

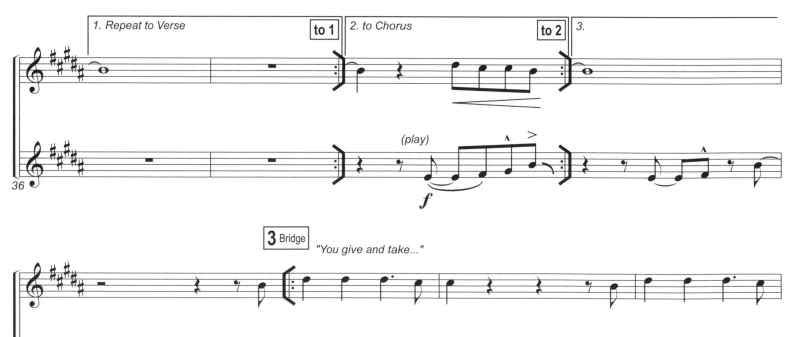

3 Bridge *"You give and take..."*

4 Chorus *"Blessed be the name..."*

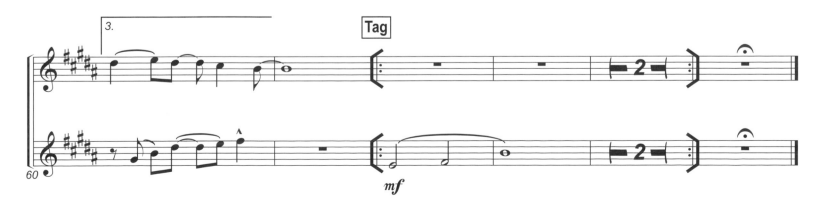

Here I Am to Worship
(Light of the World)

Bb Instruments

Words and Music by Tim Hughes
Arranged by Dan Galbraith

1. "Light of the world..."
2. "King of all days..."

"Here I am to worship..."

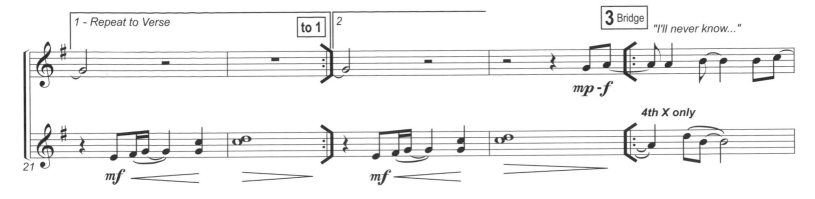

Holy Is the Lord

Bb Instruments

Words and Music by Chris Tomlin
and Louie Giglio
Arranged by Dan Galbraith

Last X to Coda ⊕

to 1

3 Bridge

"It is rising up..."

2nd X only

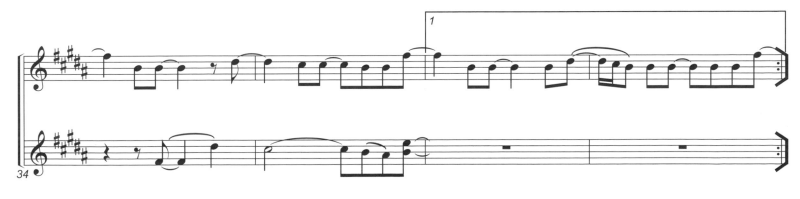

D.S. al Coda

⊕ CODA

Inst.

Mighty to Save

Bb Instruments

Words and Music by Ben Fielding
and Reuben Morgan
Arranged by Dan Galbraith

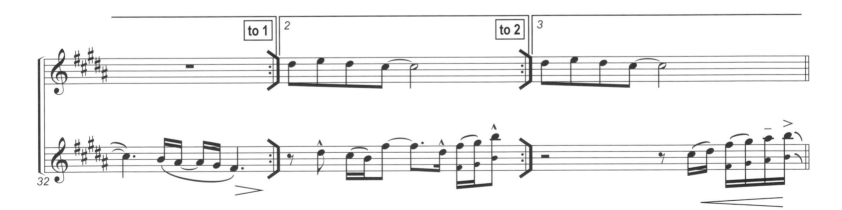

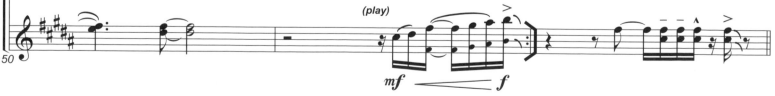

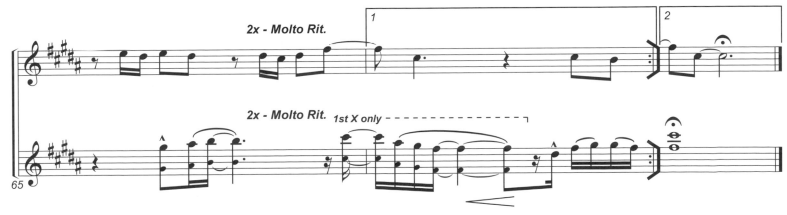

Sing to the King

Bb Instruments

Words and Music by Billy James Foote
Arranged by Dan Galbraith

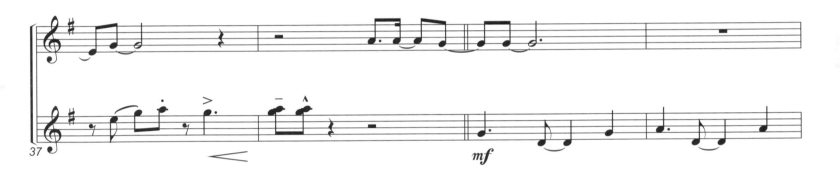

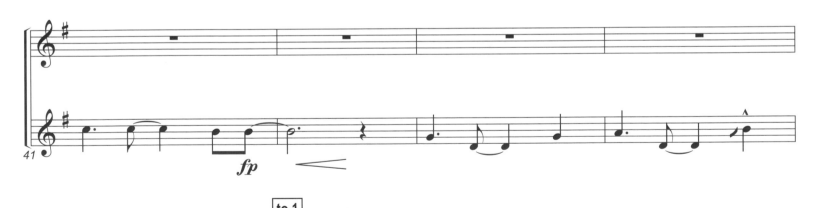

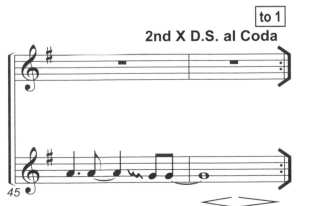

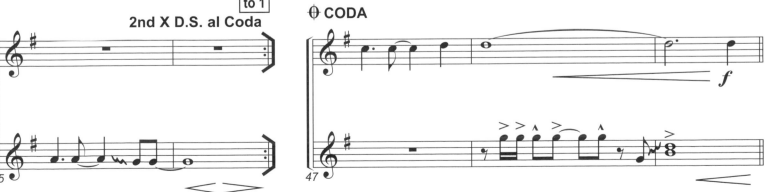

In Christ Alone

Bb Instruments

Words and Music by Keith Getty
and Stuart Townend
Arranged by Dan Galbraith

1 Verse
1. "In Christ alone my hope is found..."
2. "In Christ alone, Who took on flesh..."

3. "There in the ground..."

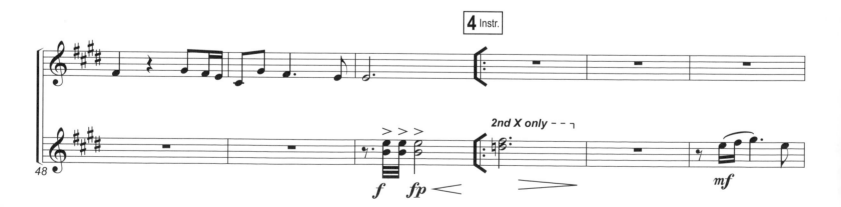

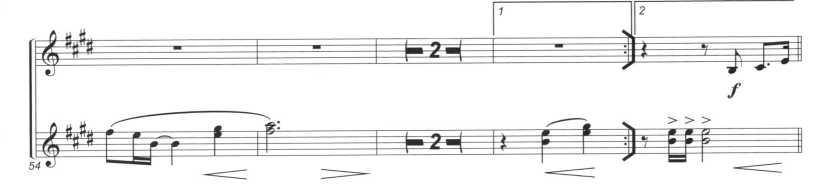

5 Verse

4. "No guilt in life..."

6 Tag

Your Name

Bb Instruments

Words and Music by Paul Baloche
and Glenn Packiam
Arranged by Dan Galbraith

4 Chorus *"Your name..."*

5 Chorus *"Your name..."*

Sacred Instrumental Collections
FROM
HAL LEONARD

HYMNS FOR THE MASTER
Book/CD Packs

15 inspirational favorites, including: All Hail the Power of Jesus' Name • Amazing Grace • Crown Him with Many Crowns • Joyful, Joyful We Adore Thee • This Is My Father's World • When I Survey the Wondrous Cross • and more.

00841136	Flute	$12.95
00841137	Clarinet	$12.95
00841138	Alto Sax	$12.95
00841139	Trumpet	$12.95
00841140	Trombone	$12.95
00841239	Piano Accomp. (No CD)	$8.95

PRAISE & WORSHIP HYMN SOLOS
Book/CD Packs

15 hymns arranged for solo performance by Stan Pethel. Includes: Blessed Be the Name • Come, Thou Fount of Every Blessing • Fairest Lord Jesus • My Faith Looks Up to Thee • To God Be the Glory • We Have Heard the Joyful Sound • more.

00841375	Alto Sax	$12.95
00841376	Clarinet/Tenor Sax	$12.95
00841378	F Horn	$12.95
00841373	Flute	$12.95
00841374	Piano Accompaniment	$8.95
00841379	Trombone/Baritone	$12.95
00841377	Trumpet	$12.95
00841380	Violin	$12.95

SOUNDS OF CELEBRATION
SOLOS WITH ENSEMBLE ARRANGEMENTS FOR TWO OR MORE PLAYERS
arr. Stan Pethel • Daybreak Music

Here's a new series useful to fill plenty of solo and ensemble needs. Whether it's a soloist using a book (accompanied by piano or the fully-orchestrated accompaniment track) or two, three, four players, or a full orchestra, *Sounds of Celebration* is a uniquely flexible new idea for church instrumentalists! Each book includes a solo line and an ensemble line. Mix and match lines with different instruments if used with an ensemble, or play the solo line when used as a solo book. Titles include: As the Deer • Give Thanks • He Is Exalted • Lord, I Lift Your Name on High • More Precious Than Silver • Shine, Jesus, Shine • Shout to the Lord • and more.

08742501	Conductor's Score (with Acc. CD)	$24.99
08742502	Flute	$5.95
08742503	Trumpet	$5.95
08742504	Clarinet	$5.99
08742505	Trombone	$5.95
08742506	Horn	$5.95
08742507	E♭ Alto Sax	$5.95
08742508	B♭ Tenor Sax	$5.95
08742509	Violin	$5.95
08742510	Cello	$5.95
08742511	Bass/Tuba	$5.95
08742512	Percussion 1, 2	$5.95
08742513	Piano/Rhythm	$9.99
08742514	Accompaniment CD	$26.99

SOUNDS OF CELEBRATION – VOLUME 2
SOLOS WITH ENSEMBLE ARRANGEMENTS FOR TWO OR MORE PLAYERS
arr. Stan Pethel • Daybreak Music

This sequel to the successful Volume One contains a wealth of popular praise choruses blended with favorite hymns. Perform with one, two, three, four or more players! Mix and match instruments regardless of your weekly attendance. Songs include: All Hail King Jesus • Find Us Faithful • Give Thanks • Be Glorified • Sanctuary • I Surrender All • Come Thou Fount • Now Thank We All Our God • and many more.

08743309	Conductor's Score	$24.99
08743310	Flute	$5.95
08743311	Trumpet	$5.95
08743312	Clarinet	$5.95
08743313	Trombone	$5.95
08743314	F Horn	$5.95
08743315	E♭ Alto Saxophone	$5.95
08743316	B♭ Tenor Saxophone	$5.95
08743317	Violin	$5.95
08743318	Cello	$5.95
08743319	Bass/Tuba	$5.95
08743320	Percussion	$5.95
08743321	Piano/Rhythm	$9.95
08743322	Accompaniment CD	$26.99

WORSHIP FAVORITES
Book/CD Packs

Features solo arrangements of 15 powerful and well-known songs. The full-accompaniment, play-along CD with tempo adjustment software lets solo instrumentalists sound just like the pros! Songs include: Agnus Dei • Great Is the Lord • He Is Exalted • Here I Am to Worship • In Christ Alone • Indescribable • Mighty to Save • There Is a Redeemer • The Wonderful Cross • and more.

00842501	Flute	$12.99
00842502	Clarinet	$12.99
00842503	Alto Sax	$12.99
00842504	Tenor Sax	$12.99
00842505	Trumpet	$12.99
00842506	Horn	$12.99
00842507	Trombone	$12.99
00842508	Violin	$12.99
00842509	Viola	$12.99
00842510	Cello	$12.99

WORSHIP SOLOS
Book/CD Packs

These book/CD packs let solo instrumentalists play with great-sounding full-band accompaniment tracks to 11 classic worship songs: Ancient of Days • Come, Now Is the Time to Worship • Draw Me Close • Firm Foundation • I Could Sing of Your Love Forever • My Life Is in You, Lord • Open the Eyes of My Heart • The Potter's Hand • Shout to the Lord • Shout to the North • We Fall Down.

00841836	Flute	$12.95
00841840	Tenor Sax	$12.95
00841841	Trumpet	$12.95
00841843	Trombone	$12.95
00841844	Violin	$12.95
00841846	Cello	$12.95
00841847	Piano Accompaniment for Winds (No CD)	$8.95
00841848	Piano Accompaniment for Strings (No CD)	$8.95

HAL•LEONARD® CORPORATION
7777 W. BLUEMOUND RD. P.O. BOX 13819 MILWAUKEE, WI 53213
www.halleonard.com

Prices, contents and availability subject to change without notice.